3.

85/8894

ABOUT THE BOOK

The careers of outstanding women in the world of tennis are examined in detail in this lively collection of biographies. Rosemary Casals, Evonne Goolagong Cawley, Margaret Court, Chris Evert, and Billy Jean King have distinct backgrounds as well as distinctive playing styles. The well-known author and feminist, Marion Meade, traces the interests of each player from early childhood to tournament competition, placing special emphasis on the style, dedication, and contribution each has made to professional tennis and to women in sports.

On the cover, clockwise from the top:
Chris Evert, Billie Jean King, Rosemary Casals,
Evonne Goolagong Cawley, Margaret Court.

WOMEN IN SPORTS

TENNIS
by Marion Meade

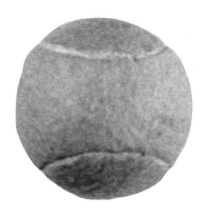

Harvey House, Publishers

New York, New York

Series Originator, Thetis Powers; Editor-in-Chief, Jeanne Gardner
Project Editor, Virginie Fowler; Designer, Kay Ward
Financing arranged by First Women's Bank, New York, New York

PICTURE CREDITS
Australian Information Service, 40, 56-57, 62, 65, 66, 68,
    77
L'eggs World Series of Women's Tennis, 17, 24, 61
Peter Travers, 15, 21, 28, 33, 43, 45
U.S. Lawn Tennis Association, and Russ Adams, 34, 47,
    54, 71, 75
Virginia Slims Championships 18, 31, 37, 50-51, jacket

For Alison

Library of Congress Catalog Card Number 75-15066
Manufactured in the United States of America
ISBN 0-8178-5402-9

Harvey House, Publishers
20 Waterside Plaza
New York, New York 10010

CONTENTS

FOREWORD

Tennis was introduced in this country by Mary Ewing Outerbridge, in 1874. While vacationing in Bermuda, Mary noticed British army officers swatting a ball back and forth across a net. Curious, she asked what they were playing.

"Lawn tennis," they said, explaining that the game had been invented the year before by an Englishman, Major Walter Wingfield.

Mary returned home to Staten Island, New York, with a package containing tennis rackets, balls, and a net. Customs officials, however, took the parcel. They thought it held dangerous weapons. It took Mary a while to get it back.

She tried to interest women friends in playing. Most of

them declined. They thought it unladylike. Just about the only ones to show an interest were her brothers.

The Outerbridges belonged to the Staten Island Cricket and Baseball Club. Mary's brothers were on the board of directors. They won permission for Mary to set up a tennis court at the club.

The new sport became popular on Staten Island. Soon it spread to other parts of the country. For years tennis was a snobbish sport played only by the rich at country clubs. This changed eventually, and today tennis is played by 13 million Americans. It is more popular than golf.

Tennis is one of the few sports that has always been played by both women and men. There have been many fine women players—Helen Wills, Alice Marble, Maureen Connolly, and Althea Gibson, the first black woman to compete.

In 1923 Helen Hotchkiss Wightman, winner of 45 national titles, established the Wightman Cup, an annual contest between women in the United States and Britain. Some compare it to the Davis Cup, awarded in men's tennis.

Even so, women players were considered second-rate. Tennis promoters insisted that spectators were not interested in watching women, so women were permitted to tag along, but were not offered big prizes.

For nearly a century, discrimination was accepted. Women were good sports. They didn't complain.

When women received attention, it was for their clothing, not for their ability. Gussie Moran became news only when she appeared on court in lace panties. Other women jazzed up the traditional white tennis dress with pink and blue hems, or embroidered kittens and butterflies on them.

Not until the 1970's did female players finally rebel. In

tennis, neither men nor women earn a salary. They must win to get paid. The prize money for women was insultingly small compared to the prizes men got.

In 1970 Billie Jean King, Rosemary Casals, and other top players went on strike, refusing to play in a United States Lawn Tennis Association (USLTA) tournament in Los Angeles. The explosion was over money. The men's singles prize was $12,500. The women's, $1,500.

Tennis promoter Gladys Heldman quickly organized a tournament in Houston for the rebels. The USLTA suspended the women. Now they could not play in any USLTA-sponsored match. It also meant they were out of work.

Virginia Slims, the cigarette manufacturers, came to their rescue by sponsoring a women's professional tennis tour. It was a beginning that became a big success. Women's tennis has been flying high ever since.

Another turning point came in 1973 when the U.S. Open Championships at Forest Hills, New York, finally offered equal prize money for men and women.

That year, Billie Jean King put women's tennis on the map. Her match against Bobby Riggs at the Houston Astrodome sparked tremendous publicity. People who had never seen a tennis match—and had never seen a woman play—watched Billie Jean's sizzling victory on television. She made people aware that women are exciting players— even more interesting than men because a woman's game relies less on power, more on skill.

There is no question that the lace-panties era in women's tennis is over. Today the emphasis is on ability. At tournaments women get the biggest cheers and sign the most autographs. People pay to see them. It's a whole new game.

THE GAME

A net is strung across a court. Players stand on opposite sides of it. If there are two players, the game is called *singles*. If there are four players (two on each side), it is called *doubles*.

The player who serves first is the *server*. The other player is the *receiver*. The server serves one entire game. After that, she becomes the receiver for a full game. For the remainder of the match, players take turns serving and receiving.

Here is how the game starts: One player stands at the rear of her side of the court, behind the base line. She positions herself to one side of the center mark. She serves the ball to her opponent.

To serve, she tosses the ball into the air over her head.

Before the ball can fall to the ground, she hits it so that it crosses over the net. It must land in the service court diagonally opposite her.

The server has two chances to make a good serve. If her first serve does not land in the correct area, it is called a *fault*. She tries again. If her second serve is not good, she has made a *double fault*. Then she loses the point.

The player who receives the serve may stand anywhere she wishes. She must let the ball bounce once—but not twice. Then she must hit the ball back over the net. She cannot hit the ball outside the court's boundary lines.

Now the game is under way. From this point on, the players may hit the ball before it bounces. This is known as a *volley*. Or they may hit it on the first bounce, which is called a *ground stroke*.

There are a variety of strokes that a player may use. One is the *lob*. This means that she sends the ball over her opponent's head. A lob is a good shot to use when your opponent is at the net.

Another stroke is the *dropshot*. This happens when a player hits the ball so that it barely clears the net.

A *backhand* stroke is used when the ball lands on the left side of a right-handed person—or on the right side of a left-hander. Chris Evert uses a two-handed backhand, gripping the racket with both hands.

Other strokes include the *smash*, *half-volley*, and *chop*.

As the game continues, the ball goes back and forth over the net until one player misses. Sometimes she makes an error by hitting the ball into the net or outside the court. Or she might fail to hit the ball on its first bounce. When she makes any of these mistakes, her opponent wins a *point*.

When a player wins a certain number of points, she wins a *game*. When she wins a certain number of games, she has won a *set*. When she wins a certain number of sets, she has won the *match*.

Points in tennis are called love, 15, 30, 40, deuce, advantage, and game.

This is how to keep score. Zero, or nothing, is called *love*. The first point won by a player is called 15. The second point won by that player is called 30. The third point is 40. The fourth point won by a player gives her the game.

If, however, each player has won 3 points (40-all), the score is *deuce*. Then the next point won by a player gives her *advantage*, but if she loses that point, the score is deuce again. In other words, if the score is 40-all, a player must win two points in a row to win the game.

The first player to win six games wins a set. However, she must be at least two games ahead of her opponent (6-3, 7-5, 8-6). Sometimes, if a set is tied at 6-all, a *tie-breaker* is played.

In women's tennis a match consists of two-out-of-three sets. The first player who wins two sets wins the match.

ONE The Old Lady: Billie Jean King

On the night of September 20, 1973, more than 30,000 fans jammed the Houston Astrodome—a record number for a tennis match. Some 50 million others watched on television around the world. Office workers in Australia took early lunch breaks to witness the event. In England, people stayed up until 3 A.M.

This was no ordinary game. It had been billed as 'The Battle of the Sexes' and 'The Match of the Century.' A sign outside the Astrodome read: THURSDAY: $100,000 WINNER TAKE ALL BILLIE JEAN KING VS. BOBBY RIGGS.

A few months earlier, Bobby Riggs had trounced Margaret Court, the Australian ace. Cocky over his win, he had challenged Billie Jean King.

Bobby was fifty-five years old. Billie Jean was twenty-nine. In tennis, youth and stamina count greatly. Would this match be fair?

Bobby thought so. "Any good male player, whatever his age, will always beat a lady," he crowed.

Once before Billie Jean had refused to play Riggs. Now

she accepted his challenge. "The match with Margaret set women and women's tennis back and I'm going to even it up," she said. "I have a cause. I guarantee I'll beat him."

Hardly anyone believed her. The odds were 8 to 5 in Riggs' favor.

"When the pressure mounts and she thinks about 50 million people watching her on TV, she'll fold," Riggs promised. "That's just the way women are."

To prepare for the match, Bobby gobbled 416 vitamin pills a day. Billie Jean was recovering from a virus. She did leg exercises and rested.

On the night of the match the Astrodome looked like a Roman circus. A trumpet sounded. The band struck up a feminist tune, 'I Am Woman.' Billie Jean made her entrance in a red and gold Roman litter, borne by four bare-chested males. Like Cleopatra, she was carried over a golden carpet to the center of the arena. Her blue and green tennis dress sparkled with rhinestones. The audience burst into wild applause.

Bobby rode into the arena in a Chinese rickshaw pulled by eight women in red shorts. The band played, 'Anything You Can Do, I Can Do Better.'

Before the contest started, Billie Jean and Bobby exchanged gifts. Since he acted like a 'male chauvinist pig,' she gave him a live baby pig wearing a pink ribbon. Bobby presented her with a gigantic caramel sucker and said she was 'the biggest sucker in the world' for daring to play him.

Then the clowning stopped and the match began. They agreed to play by the rules for men's tennis: the first to take three sets out of five would win. Billie Jean served first. Back and forth the ball spun. Bobby sent her high lobs, the

kind for which he is famous. But Billie Jean smashed the ball right back over his head.

She won the first game easily. To her surprise, Bobby seemed slow. She thought he was faking. At the first rest she asked her coach, "He's putting me on, right?"

Her coach said, "No."

She won the first set, 6-4. Bobby used every shot he

knew, but he couldn't stop Billie Jean. He chased from one side of the court to the other. Much of the time, he never got a chance to hit the ball.

Billie Jean took the second set, 6-3. The women in the Astrodome roared happily. Most of the men looked glum. The baby pig had fallen asleep.

By this time it was clear that Bobby was in trouble. He took an 'injury break' for hand cramps. Slumped in a chair on the sidelines, he gulped another handful of vitamins.

"Come on, Billie Jean," shouted a man in the audience. "Start acting feminine—miss a few!"

Finally in the third set, Bobby double-faulted and found himself facing match point. This was the crucial moment. Billie Jean needed only one more point to win. As Bobby served, the crowd leaped to its feet. There was a short volley. Then Bobby sent a backhand into the net.

A wooden object sailed toward the roof—Billie Jean's racket. The electronic scoreboard flashed 6-3. *The Battle of the Sexes* was over.

Afterward, somebody asked Billie Jean what her victory meant.

"Maybe it means that people will start to respect women athletes," she said. "Not just me. There are plenty more to take my place."

When Billie Jean Moffit was growing up, all the athletic heroes were men. She was the biggest kid in her class at Los Cerritos Elementary School in California. She was also the best athlete—and that included boys, too. When people called her a *tomboy*, she didn't like it. She wished there were another name for girls who loved sports.

Billie Jean played football in front of her house on West 36th Street in Long Beach. She also liked basketball, softball, and track. By the time she was ten, she was playing shortstop on a girls' softball team.

"Sis," her mother said, "I'm not raising a halfback or a shortstop. You'll have to find a more ladylike sport."

One day Billie Jean asked her father for advice. He thought for a while. "Well, there are three good sports for girls," he said, "golf, swimming, and tennis."

"Golf is too slow," Billie Jean objected. "There's too much walking and not enough action." Swimming didn't appeal to her either. She didn't swim well. Besides, spending a lot of time in the water sounded boring.

"What's tennis?" she asked, having only a vague idea of the game.

"You run a lot and hit the ball," her father explained. "I think you'd like it."

She wasn't sure, but she decided to try.

There was a problem. She needed a racket and the cheapest cost eight dollars. Billie Jean began doing odd jobs for the neighbors. She put the money in a jar. The dimes and quarters mounted up until she had earned most of the money. Then she grew impatient.

"I've got to have that racket," she told her mother. "I've just got to have it."

Finally her parents gave her the rest of the money and they all went downtown while Billie Jean picked out a racket. It had maroon nylon strings and a maroon handle.

A few days later, a classmate asked if she wanted to play. Billie Jean lost, 6-0, 6-0. She was furious with herself because she hadn't been able to hit the ball at all.

A tennis teacher named Clyde Walker worked for the city's Recreation Department. Once a week he gave free lessons at Houghton Park near Billie Jean's home. Mr. Walker showed her how to grip the racket and how to drop the ball and swing at it.

"All right, Billie Jean," he said, "now you try."

She dropped the ball and swung. To her surprise, she hit it over the net. Several hours later her mother picked her up in their old Chevy convertible. "How was it?" she asked.

"Great!" said Billie Jean. "Just great. I want to play tennis forever. I'm going to be the Number One tennis player in the whole world."

"That's nice, dear," said her mother and drove home.

Betty Moffit wasn't too excited. Six months earlier her daughter had been equally enthusiastic about piano lessons. She had pleaded, "I'll just die if you don't get me a piano." Now that she had discovered tennis, she didn't want to play the piano anymore.

"No piano, no tennis," her mother said firmly. "You can't begin a project and drop it, Sissy. I want you to see things through."

Billie Jean's family didn't have much money. Her father, Bill, was a fireman with the Long Beach Fire Department. To make ends meet, her mother worked as an Avon representative, selling cosmetics.

All the Moffits were sports fans. Billie Jean's father played baseball and basketball. Her mother was an excellent swimmer. Her little brother Randy loved baseball. Randy became a pitcher for the San Francisco Giants.

Once Billie Jean began learning tennis, she thought about nothing else. Nearly every day her mother drove her to one of the parks where Clyde Walker gave lessons. At night she pounded a ball against the redwood fence in her backyard. The neighbors complained about the noise. One evening the fence collapsed. Her father had to replace it with a cement wall.

At eleven, she played her first tournament at the Los Angeles Tennis Club. She felt awed because the club was a fancy place. Right away she saw that the other kids in the tournament had money and she didn't. They could buy hamburgers and french fries at the clubhouse. She brought her lunch in a paper bag.

Afterward, the players lined up for a group picture. The director of the tournament pointed to Billie Jean. "Not you," he said. "You can't be in the picture because you're not properly dressed."

Billie Jean was wearing her usual outfit—white shorts and a white T-shirt. But the director expected boys to wear shorts and girls to wear tennis dresses. Billie Jean was angry and embarrassed.

"What silly people!" she thought. "They should care about how you play—not how you look."

She never forgot that first tournament. She vowed to change tennis someday. It was too stuffy.

In summer most kids slept late and took it easy. Not Billie Jean. She got up at 8:00 A.M. and practiced all morning. After a lunch break, she played until dinner. During the school year, she walked the four miles to high school to toughen her body.

Her hard work brought results. She played in junior tournaments all over southern California. When she was

fifteen, tennis fans in her hometown raised the money to send her to the national girls championship at Middletown, Ohio. She lost in the quarterfinals. She often lost at first but then she began to win. By her sixteenth birthday, she ranked #19 in the national ratings for women.

At seventeen, she zoomed to fourth place. That year she missed her high school graduation and went to England instead to play at Wimbledon, the world's most famous tennis tournament. She and eighteen-year-old Karen Krantze won the doubles championship—the youngest team to do so in Wimbledon's history.

In both England and the United States, tennis fans cheered Billie Jean. She was a chubby girl of 5'4½" who weighed 140 pounds. With her glasses, short brown hair, and upturned nose, she looked like the girl-next-door. The crowds loved her because she acted natural on the court. When she missed a point, she scolded herself. "Keep your eye on the ball, stupid!" she'd mutter. Or she'd growl, "Nuts!"

Tennis was becoming her whole life. Still, she didn't plan to make it her career. She entered Los Angeles State College as a history major. For the next three years, she followed the same routine: in the summer she went to Wimbledon, and played tournaments in the United States; every September she put her racket in mothballs and returned to college.

In her sophomore year she met Larry King, a pre-law student at Los Angeles State. Billie Jean says he has been the biggest influence in her life. Larry encouraged her to make some decisions about tennis. Did she want to continue college or did she want to be the world's best woman tennis player? If so, she had to play every day, not just a few months of the year.

In 1963 she faced bitter disappointment. She had reached the final at Wimbledon, only to be beaten by Margaret Court (then Margaret Smith) of Australia.

"I know you could win," Margaret said to her after the match. "But I always wear you out. You just don't play enough."

Three weeks after Billie Jean and Larry became engaged, she left college and went to Australia to take lessons from Mervyn Rose, a renowned coach. For three months she did daily exercises and tennis drills. When she came home she was in top physical condition. Her game showed it, too.

In 1965, the year she and Larry were married, she didn't lose a single match in the United States. Two years later she won both the U.S. and Wimbledon titles for singles, doubles, and mixed doubles. At last she was world champion—Number One.

However, Billie Jean didn't think she would play much longer—maybe three or four more years. She would retire and have children and settle down as the wife of a successful lawyer. It did not turn out that way, for tennis was on the brink of a revolution that would change the game, and Billie Jean would be a leader in that revolution.

Before 1968 you had to be an amateur to play at Wimbledon and Forest Hills. Then a rules change permitted professionals to play, too. Top tennis stars like Billie Jean "turned pro," and now played for money instead of for trophies.

The prize money for men and women, however, was unequal. Women players thought this unfair. Billie Jean, always outspoken, led the battle. She spoke out strongly for a fairer share of prize money. She filed petitions, threatened boycotts, and staged walkouts. She helped to organize a women's tennis circuit, the Virginia Slims.

Billie Jean's ambition was to earn $100,000 a year. It wasn't just the money. "This country is oriented toward professional sports," she said in 1971, when she became the first female athlete to earn $100,000. "I wanted to show the world that women can earn a good living in sports. It'll open up more avenues for women in other sports."

At 31, Billie Jean was known among tennis players as 'The Old Lady.' She had been playing for over twenty years, and seven times had been Number One. She again won the Women's Singles title at Wimbledon in 1975, beating Evonne Goolagong Cawley.

In recent years, Billie Jean has broadened her interests. She has a four-year contract to play for the New York Sets, part of a new pro tennis league called World Team Tennis. She publishes a monthly magazine, *WomanSports*. And she is a TV sportscaster.

Billie Jean King is one of the most famous women athletes in the world. Even though she says she has hung up her racket so far as big singles competitions go, she will be remembered as a pioneer of women's rights on the tennis court.

TWO Rosebud: Rosemary Casals

"Please let me hit the ball, Daddy," eight-year-old Rosie begged. It was a crisp Sunday morning at the public tennis courts in San Francisco's Golden Gate Park. Every weekend Rosie's father played doubles here with his friends. For months his pint-sized daughter had been pestering, "Take me along."

"All right," he finally agreed. "You can come and watch."

At the park Rosie sat quietly for a while. Tennis looked like fun, but she soon grew bored watching the men hit the ball back and forth over the net.

"Daddy, when are you going to play with me?" she kept calling out. The men kept right on hitting the ball.

"If I ask often enough," Rosie thought, "I bet he'll let me play." But her plan didn't work. What's more, she sensed that the men didn't like being pestered. One of her father's friends strolled over. He fished a quarter out of his pocket. "Here, honey," he said, kindly but firmly. "Why don't you take a ride on the merry-go-round?"

That was not the end of Rosie's ambition to play tennis. Her father soon realized that she really wanted to learn the game, so he began teaching her the basics. Seven months later she played in her first tournament forty miles away at San Leandro—and won.

That year she began to play in all the junior tournaments near her home. Before long she was rated Number One among her age-group in California.

"I want to be good," she would tell herself fiercely. "I want to be the best."

People who watched little Rosie said that she was a born tennis player. Even today she and the Australian champion, Evonne Goolagong, are said to have more natural ability than any of the other women tennis players alive. It is also said that Rosie knows better than most how to use her talent.

In recent years Rosemary Casals has been rated as one of the best half-dozen female players in the world. Until September 20, 1973, however, few Americans had heard of her. On that night, Bobby Riggs played Billie Jean King, Rosie's close friend.

For a change, Rosie was not on the court. Along with ABC-TV's Howard Cosell and tennis pro, Gene Scott, she was in the broadcasting booth, hired by ABC to comment on the match. While Billie Jean trounced Bobby, Rosie kept up a patter of sharp, funny, and extremely honest remarks. Her performance outdid Howard Cosell's, a man known as a master of the put-down.

After the King-Riggs match, Rosie's name became a household word. Most of the words weren't favorable

though. People called her unladylike, uncouth, and a loud-mouth. Some mistakenly thought she was Howard Cosell's daughter because their last names sounded similar. They dismissed her as a chip off the old block. Others admired her spunk.

For months thereafter, whenever she played a match, audiences greeted her with a chorus of boos. "Hey Rosie," the hecklers would shout, "where's Howard?"

The television appearance gave Rosie a bad name with the public, but it helped her career. People grew curious about the intense young woman whose trademark is a head-band holding back her black hair. "Who is Rosie Casals?" they asked. "Where has she been?"

Rosemary was born September 16, 1948, in San Francisco. Of Spanish descent, she is a grandniece of the late, world-famous cellist, Pablo Casals. Her parents lived in Central America in San Salvador, emigrating to San Francisco before Rosie was born. Manuel Casals ran a small stamp-machine business. Once he had been an excellent soccer player, but after suffering an injury while playing, he turned to tennis instead.

In school Rosie was a bright student. She loved reading. But after she discovered tennis, her interest in books faded. By the time she entered George Washington High School, she had been winning tournaments for several years.

Her teachers wanted to know why she didn't do her homework. "Tennis is my life," she would explain. "You have to understand that school comes second for me."

She began to do poorly in her studies, mostly because she was never in school. She was on a tennis court.

One day the high school tennis team invited her to become a member. "No thanks," she said. And she said to herself, "It would be a waste of time."

By her sixteenth birthday she had won every trophy in California. It was time, she decided, to compete nationally and internationally. Soon Rosie was rated #14 among the top twenty female players in the country.

One of the first to notice her talent was another Califor-

nian. When Rosie was seventeen, she received a call from Billie Jean King. "Are you interested in being my doubles partner at Forest Hills this year?" Billie Jean asked.

Would she! Forest Hills isn't just any tennis tournament. In the United States, it is THE tournament. Rosie was thrilled and honored. She knew she'd be a good partner for Billie Jean.

Rosie believed that she had the ability to become a top player, maybe even Number One, but one thing worried her—her height. She had stopped growing at five-feet, two-and-one-quarter inches. "Billie Jean is only two inches taller than me," she'd fret, "but look how much difference it makes."

Eventually Rosie and Billie Jean became known as the world's best women's doubles team. Together they won five Wimbledon titles as well as many other titles in this country.

In some ways this was good for Rosie—in other ways not so good. At seventeen, she blossomed into an international star. Since she was young and tiny, the newspapers and fans nicknamed her Rosebud. They praised her courage on the court.

They also began thinking of her as Billie Jean's doubles partner—not as a personality in her own right. Possibly this affected Rosie's career, for she has yet to become Number One. At one time or another, she has beaten all the top players—Margaret Court, Billie Jean King, Virginia Wade, and Nancy Richey Gunter. She has earned a reputation for being a good runner-up who gives the champs a hard time, but who usually loses in the end.

"I started early and I was always lumped together with

'The Old Lady,' and Margaret, and Nancy Gunter," Rosie once said. "But they have been playing tennis five or six years longer than I have. It's kinda' tough getting recognition when you're always hanging around with the best."

In 1968, at twenty, Rosie became one of the first women players to turn pro. She signed a contract to play a tour of France, but found that being a professional wasn't glamorous at all.

"We rode trains all day and played every night," she recalls. "There were times when we would get to a place and the court wasn't even laid down yet. There were no tennis balls."

Despite hardships, Rosie does not regret becoming a pro. She went on to win more than thirty national titles. Twice she has been a finalist at Forest Hills. As the prize money has steadily mounted, Rosie has cashed in, becoming one of the world's top money-winners.

In 1973 she earned over $115,000. That year she won the biggest single prize in the history of women's sports, the *Family Circle Tournament*. She defeated Nancy Gunter— 3-6, 6-1, 7-5—and took home a check for $30,000.

"Miss Casals has had many brilliant moments in her international career," wrote *The New York Times*, "but never has she displayed such commitment to purpose and concentration as she did during this four-day tournament."

Along with her friend, Billie Jean, Rosie has done much for the growth of women's tennis. In 1970 Rosie and Billie Jean led a group of women who threatened to boycott future tournaments. Protesting against discrimination, they demanded bigger prizes. They also asked that women's matches be given the same spotlight as men's.

"They schedule us at noon, or real late, or on an outside court," Rosie complained. "To me, that's real crummy."

The protests paid off. Women were given a better deal and more money. As a result, they began to attract larger crowds.

The life of a professional tennis player can be exhausting. There is constant travel, hotels, late hours, and the grind of playing night after night.

"I love this life," says Rosie, "even though it's not all as glamorous and exciting as people think. I don't like sleeping in airplanes and getting in and out of airports at three o'clock in the morning."

Still, she has no plans for settling down. She enjoys being single. "Marriage is not my ultimate goal," she explains frankly. "I like to do as I please, and come and go as I want. I'm happy being my own boss."

When she isn't touring, she lives in a $75,000 home in Sausalito, just outside San Francisco. There she plays her drums or guitar. Sometimes she writes poetry.

Her idea of relaxation is to drop in at a McDonald's for her favorite meal, a Big Mac and a milkshake. She owns two horses, four cats, two sports cars, and several bikes. She loves beer, smokes an occasional cigar, and wears embroidered jeans with expensive Gucci belts.

Practicing tennis bores her. When she's on tour, she'll fly into a town in the middle of the night. A few hours later, she'll be on the court. After a five-minute warm-up, she's ready to play.

During a match, Rosie's face is a picture of grim determination. She never smiles. "What's so funny about killing yourself on the tennis court?" she says. "It's hard work."

Her big strength is speed. She has the fastest legs in tennis today. She has to be quick. It takes her five or six steps to get to a ball that taller players can reach in two steps.

On court and off, Rosie's style is brash. That's why she is such an exciting player to watch. Because she has a flair for the spectacular, she has brought fire and color to the game. An outrageous ham at times, she will return shots while lying flat on the court. Sometimes she makes returns from behind her back or even from between her legs.

Usually tennis fans are not noisy. Their applause is polite. But they don't applaud for twenty-six-year-old Rosie Casals. They cheer until their throats get hoarse. Or they boo loudly. That's the kind of razzle-dazzle game she plays.

THREE Cinderella In Sneakers: Chris Evert

"**Of** course I'll never win the championship," Chris thought as she arrived at the West Side Tennis Club in Forest Hills, New York, on a hot September day in 1971. This was her first time playing in an important tournament like the U.S. Open Championships.

Her stomach fluttered with butterflies. The previous year, when she was fifteen, she had played a few big stars like Margaret Court. To her great shock, she had beaten them.

Still, she felt tense. Top players like Margaret and Billie Jean scared her. After all, they were almost old enough to be her mother.

Another thing worried her. She wasn't used to playing on grass. Back home in Fort Lauderdale, Florida, she played on clay courts. No, she didn't have a chance to win the Women's National Championship. The most she hoped was to win a few matches.

"Competing at Forest Hills will be good for me," she thought. "How can I find out if I'm any good unless I play against the best?"

Her first opponent was Edda Buding from West Germany. Chris had no trouble whipping her, 6-1, 6-0. The 10,000 spectators in the stands applauded politely.

Her second match was against Mary Ann Eisel of St. Louis, a seasoned professional. She looked at Chris across the net and saw a sweet little girl with pigtails and ribbons. Surely she could beat a sixteen-year-old amateur.

For a while it looked as if Mary Ann would win easily. She sent Chris chasing all over the court. The first set went to Mary Ann, 6-4.

In the second set, Mary Ann had Chris on the run again. Then something happened. Chris began to fight back. Six times they reached match point—the moment when a winning final point can wrap up the match—but Mary Ann couldn't make the point she needed.

By now the nerve-wracking contest had the crowd's full attention. The set was tied, 6-6. To break the tie, they played one more game. Chris won it, taking the set 7-6.

Mary Ann, crestfallen, seemed to crumple. A few minutes later it was all over. Chris won the third set, 6-1. The match was hers. Leaving the court, she received a roaring ovation from the audience.

From then on, Chris Evert was the sweetheart of Forest Hills. The audiences loved her. They cheered her, and they applauded whenever her opponents made a mistake.

Next Chris defeated Françoise Durr of France. Then she went on to beat Australia's Lesley Hunt. Finally she found herself in the semifinals. If she won, she would have a crack at the championship.

Chris's opponent was none other than Billie Jean King, queen of women's tennis. She had played Billie Jean once

before at the Virginia Slims Masters, and had won by default. Due to leg cramps, Billie Jean had been forced to drop out in the second set, so that match didn't really count.

Now, however, Billie Jean's legs were fine. It took her only two sets to polish off Chris. She beat her 6-3, 6-2. Then Billie Jean went on to defeat Rosie Casals for the championship.

Chris had been the youngest semifinalist in the history of the women's championship. Still, she felt awful about losing.

"I don't think I was ever in the match," she said afterward. "I was happy to get into the semifinals but I wasn't happy with that match. I guess I just wasn't ready to beat Billie Jean."

Five months later, Chris was ready. She played Billie Jean in a tournament in Fort Lauderdale. Before a cheering hometown crowd, she routed the champion, 6-1, 6-0.

"I don't ever remember being beaten so badly," admitted Billie Jean later.

After Forest Hills, Chris became the most popular player in tennis. The fans, especially youngsters, adored her. After a match, kids would mob her on the court while the loudspeaker blared, "Children, please. Chrissie will sign all your autographs. Just line up by the referee's porch."

Tournament officials always put her on the center court. If they didn't, fans practically tore down the place just to get a look at her. "That little shrimp is magic," commented a tennis official.

Much of her magic is in her cool style. Nothing seems to distract her. She always acts utterly poised.

Chris has two big assets. One is her two-handed back-

hand. The other is her ability to outlast her opponents. Usually she stays on the back line. When her opponent comes to the net, Chris likes to lob a ball right over her head. Or she places an accurate ground stroke past her.

Other players say that playing Chris Evert is like playing against a wall. The ball always comes back.

Adding to her cool image is Chris's appearance. She wears her long blond hair parted in the middle and pulled back at her neck with a ribbon. Sometimes she wears pigtails. Every hair is in place. Her ribbon always matches her dress. Her socks match her ribbon.

In her pierced ears are gold earrings. She wears nail polish, eyeliner, and mascara. "I feel it's important to look feminine on the court," she says. "Just because I'm an athlete doesn't mean I can't look pretty."

Some sportswriters nicknamed her 'Cinderella in Sneakers,' but others began to say that she had no emotions. They called her 'The Ice Dolly' or 'The Ball Machine,' making her sound dull and mechanical. Chris was angry.

She knew she wasn't a born athlete like Billie Jean, but she wasn't a robot either. She was steady and she worked hard at her game.

"I don't show my emotions on court," she says. "I don't want 10,000 people to see me blow my top. But off court, I cry like anybody else."

Christine Marie Evert was born into a tennis family on December 21, 1954. Her father, Jimmy Evert, was a tennis star at Notre Dame. For many years he has managed the Holiday Park Tennis Center in Fort Lauderdale, where he also teaches tennis.

Chris has an older brother and three younger brothers and sisters. They all play tennis well. Jeanne, three years younger than Chris, is a ranking woman player.

Looking back, Chris says that her whole life has been tennis. Each Evert child began playing around the age of five. This happened because Jimmy Evert's busiest days as a tennis teacher were Saturdays and Sundays. Every weekend he had to be away from his family. He didn't like it, so he asked his wife Colette to bring the kids to Holiday Park—just a few blocks from their house.

The Evert children began by hitting balls against a wall. When Jimmy Evert saw they had talent, he started giving them lessons. At first Chris had no particular love for the game.

"It was just something nice to do," she recalls.

After a few years, however, she began spending more and more time at the courts. She'd practice several hours after school. Soon she was entering junior tournaments. Before she knew it, she was playing stars like Virginia Wade and Billie Jean King.

"The idea of producing tennis champions was the farthest thing from our minds," says Chris's mother. But when the Everts saw how well their youngsters were doing, they wanted to help them become the best.

While Chris was attending St. Thomas Aquinas High School, there were strict training rules in the Evert household—four hours of practice after school, three hours on weekends, four hours daily during the summers—and balanced meals of meat, potatoes, and vegetables, early bedtimes, and no slumber parties, because athletes need rest.

The world's most important tennis tournament takes place each summer at Wimbledon, England. Kings and queens sit in the royal box. Players from all over the world come to compete. Wimbledon symbolizes the best in tennis. When she was seventeen, Chris decided to enter.

The previous year, the Wimbledon title had been won by a nineteen-year-old Australian girl, Evonne Goolagong. People said a match between Evonne and Chris would be a dream match between two brilliant newcomers.

Excitement ran high as the two players met in the semifinals. Unless Evonne beat Chris, she would not be able to play in the final. She would lose her chance to keep the title. If Chris won, *she* might go on to become champion.

It was a long match, lasting over an hour and a half. Chris took the lead. She won the first set, 6-4. In the second set, she was leading 3-0. It began to look as if Evonne would be wiped out. On the brink of defeat, Evonne shook herself awake. She began to skim over the court. She hit balls that seemed out of reach. Then, to great bursts of applause from the galleries, Evonne went on to take the match, 4-6, 6-3, 6-4.

A few weeks later, Chris and Evonne met again in the Bonne Bell Cup competition. This time Chris was determined to prove she could beat Evonne. And she did—6-3, 4-6, 6-0. A few months later they met once more at the U.S. Clay-Court Tennis Championships. Chris smashed Evonne in two sets, 7-6, 6-1. She won the championship.

By now Chris had beaten the best players and won many tournaments, including first prize in the Virginia Slims Championships. But she'd had to refuse the $25,000 purse.

Chris Evert's famous two-handed backhand stroke.

In fact, she had not been able to keep any of the thousands of dollars she had won. She was an amateur and amateurs are ineligible for cash. Instead she took home trophies. Over 250 of them were on the shelves in her bedroom.

On her eighteenth birthday, Chris turned pro. From then on, she has been one of the biggest money-winners in tennis. In 1973 she earned $152,000; the following year, over $200,000.

In 1973 Chris graduated from high school with honors, but chose tennis over college. "These are my prime years for tennis," she said. "For me, college would be a waste of time. For a couple of weeks, I think I'd enjoy college, but then I know I'd get bored."

Her life on the pro tennis circuit was anything but boring. Between playing matches and practicing, she became engaged to twenty-year-old Jimmy Connors. The romance was front-page news. Connors now ranks Number One among male players.

The engagement lasted only a year, however. "I think we both chose our careers," explained Chris. "That means more to us than marriage."

In 1974 Chris had her finest season. First she won the Italian, French, and Canadian championships. When she arrived at Wimbledon in June, she had already won 35 consecutive victories. If she reached the finals, she wondered who she'd be facing. Billie Jean, who had won the previous year? Evonne?

Chris breezed through the quarterfinals and semifinals. Billie Jean and Evonne, however, were knocked out. The title would be fought between Chris and Russia's Olga Morozova. Olga was a friend of Chris's. They had often been doubles partners.

Chris walked out on the court wearing her engagement ring, earrings, necklace, and polished fingernails. With murderous calm, she proceeded to demolish Olga. It took Chris only 59 minutes and two sets to put away her opponent. The score: 6-0, 6-4. The new world's champion took home $20,000 and a Triumph car.

"I never expected to win Wimbledon this year," Chris said after her triumphant victory. "I was thinking maybe in two or three years, when Billie Jean and Margaret Court retire."

Even though she is Number One, Chris still tries to improve her serve and volley. She never stops working. "According to some of the letters I get," she says, "kids seem to think that being a pro tennis player is all fun and games. But if you want to be champion, you've got to dedicate most of your time to tennis. Not to fooling around."

Chris has said that she plans to play for another six or seven years. Then she wants to marry and have three children.

"There are a lot of things more important than tennis," she insists. "Marriage and family are more important. So is religion—and love. I mean, if I don't get married, what am I going to do when I'm thirty?"

FOUR The Panther: Evonne Goolagong

The tiny town of Barellan in the farm country of Australia has a population of 450 people, most of whom raise wheat and sheep. The streets are largely unpaved. It is an unlikely setting to produce a world-famous tennis star, but Barellan is Evonne Goolagong's hometown.

It was a good place to grow up. The Goolagongs were poor, and the eight children did not have bicycles like other kids had, but there was enough to eat and plenty to do.

The family lived in a run-down house on the edge of town. It was small and crowded. The Goolagong children spent most of their time outdoors, fishing and swimming and climbing up into the wheat silos to hunt pigeons.

Evonne's family background includes aborigines. These people were the first to live in Australia. When white settlers arrived two hundred years ago, they took away the aborigines' land and killed large numbers of them. Like the American Indians, the aborigines suffered cruel discrimination. Even in recent times, they had to sit in special sections of movie theaters.

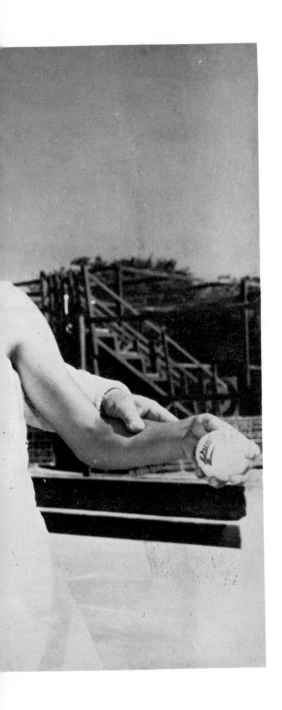

*Sixteen-year-old Evonne
Goolagong in 1967
with her coach Victor
Edwards, when she was
in her third year
in high school.*

The Goolagongs are the only part aboriginal family in Barellan, but they are treated the same as everyone else. Ken Goolagong, Evonne's father, is a sheepshearer.

Even as a child, Evonne loved sports. Her mother remembers that she never liked dolls. Instead, Evonne played with an old tennis ball. Before she was a year old, she held it in her hand and squeezed it. As a toddler, she bounced the ball and hit it with a broomstick. Some small children carry around a blanket. Evonne was *never* without her tennis ball. She was good at any game which involved running and jumping. But tennis interested her most.

Even though Barellan is a small village, it has fine tennis courts. Evonne began hanging around the Barellan War Memorial Tennis Club. She would hit a ball with a wooden bat. Or she earned spending money chasing balls for players.

Sometimes one of the club members would lend her a racket. Then she would practice after everyone had gone home. When she was nine, her aunt gave her a racket as a present. She slept with it. Then one of her sisters burned it. Evonne cried for days.

Bill Kurtzman, president of the tennis club, gave her another racket. He was the first person to see that she had talent. He began to teach her how to play. One day he let her take home an old net and told her to practice.

The next year Kurtzman enrolled Evonne in a touring tennis school. The traveling school was owned by Vic Edwards, a coach who runs Australia's largest tennis school. One of the men with the school noticed Evonne. Excited, he telephoned Vic Edwards in Sydney, 400 miles away.

"There's this aboriginal kid here," he reported. "She just flows around the court. She's the kind of 'natural' you see once in a long time. Of course she doesn't know how to make her shots, but she's always in the right place."

Edwards drove to Barellan to watch Evonne play. Then he visited the Goolagong home. Evonne felt shy with strangers. She ran into her room and pulled the blankets over her head. When she came out, she said hardly a word.

"What do you want to be when you grow up?" Edwards asked her.

Evonne shrugged.

"Maybe a nurse," she finally mumbled. "I haven't really thought about it."

Edwards advised her to keep practicing. He promised to return the next summer. "I'll wait and see if she keeps at the game," he thought. "So often it's just a passing interest with kids."

Evonne practiced steadily. When Edwards arrived the following year, he was impressed. He asked her parents if he could take her to Sydney for a few months. He wanted to give her lessons and enter her in tournaments. She would live with his family.

The Goolagongs agreed and off she went. She reached the semifinals of the first tournament in which she played.

Vic Edwards admired her grace on the court. He liked the way she hit the ball—real hard in the center of the racket. She had one beautiful shot, a backhand volley, that she had invented herself.

"Her main fault," decided Edwards, "is a tendency to let her mind wander. And she lacks a killer instinct."

If an opponent she had beaten started to cry, Evonne

would put her arms around the girl. Sometimes she even cried a little herself.

For the next two years Evonne spent her summer holidays in Sydney. She stayed with Vic Edwards and his wife and five daughters. They lived in a beautiful home in the suburbs. Evonne had never seen such a house before, but after several years she felt very much at home there.

At thirteen, Evonne started to attract attention—partly because of her race, but mostly due to her skill and power. She won the championship for girls under fifteen.

One thing was clear to Vic Edwards: if Evonne was going to develop into a champion, she must leave Barellan. He asked her parents if he could adopt Evonne. He would raise her as his own daughter and make her a tennis star. They said yes.

When she was fourteen, Evonne moved to Sydney. She attended high school with Edwards' daughter, Patricia. Each day after school Evonne took lessons in speech and manners. Edwards wanted her to be poised and polished. Later, when she finished high school, he sent her to secretarial school. Someday she might need a useful trade.

With each passing year Evonne improved her game. By the time she was eighteen, she had won every singles championship in Australia. Vic Edwards decided that she was ready to compete abroad.

In 1970 he took her to Europe. She went to France, Holland, England, and Germany, and won seven titles.

In England she saw snow for the first time. She ran around scraping snow off the cars. "I was trying to get enough snow to build a snowman," she says, "but there just wasn't enough. People thought I was crazy."

Evonne Goolagong at nineteen.

Her first visit to Wimbledon was a disaster. "All the people and the atmosphere got me all tensed up," she said. "I walked around with my head down. I was too scared to look up."

Evonne was knocked out in her first match by Peaches Bartkowicz of the United States. She had been so frightened that she could hardly hold her racket.

The next year, however, she won her biggest victory so far. She defeated her childhood idol, Margaret Court. In a suitcase at home in Barellan is a photograph showing Evonne at eleven, looking up at Margaret with adoring eyes.

After she beat Margaret, Vic Edwards made a prediction that Evonne would become Wimbledon champion by 1974. People didn't listen to him—they laughed. Edwards was wrong. Evonne didn't win Wimbledon in three years. She won it the very next year.

In June, 1971, Evonne visited Wimbledon again. This time she did not feel so shy. She was to play Margaret Court in the final. Margaret, of course, was favored to win, but Evonne defeated her in two sets, 6-4, 6-1. The crowd gave Evonne a standing ovation. At nineteen, she was the Number One player in the world.

Evonne felt as if she were dreaming. "I'm still in a daze," she said afterward. "I don't think I've waked up yet. I never thought I'd reach the finals, let alone win."

That night she received a silver trophy at the Wimbledon Ball. After the dance, she celebrated with friends at a London nightclub. The next day she mailed a postcard to her family, "Dear Gang, The ball was beautiful."

All of Barellan had watched her on television. People

said it was the greatest day in the town's history. They stayed up until 2 A.M. to watch her win. "She's our girl!" they cheered.

After Wimbledon Evonne rose like a meteor to world fame. Queen Elizabeth made her a member of the British Empire, one of the highest honors in Great Britain. After the ceremony, Evonne was asked what the Queen had said to her. She couldn't remember. She had been so thrilled that she forgot to pay attention.

Suddenly losing her concentration is Evonne's biggest weakness on the court. "My mind goes walkabout," she says. She explains that 'walkabout' is an aboriginal term. It means 'to wander.' "I just have these lapses," she says. "I guess I'm stuck with it. But I play better when I get behind. I say to myself, 'Now I have to play well.' "

In 1973 Evonne reached the finals in three world championships. She won the Italian tournament, but lost to Margaret Court at Forest Hills and at the Australian Open.

The next year she defeated Chris Evert to win the Australian title. The first set went all the way to a tie-breaker. Evonne won it, 7-6. Chris bounced back to take the second set, 6-4. Then Evonne pulled out all the stops. She took the third set, 6-0. Her playing had been remarkable.

A few months later she played in the third annual Virginia Slims Championship. Once again her opponent in the final was Chris Evert. Evonne won the match, 6-3, 6-4. She walked off with a check for $32,000. It was the biggest prize in the history of women's sports.

Evonne is known for her graceful style on the court. She seems to move almost like a panther. Her playing appears effortless.

Evonne Goolagong and coach Victor Edwards.

Unlike most players, Evonne is willing to hit every ball. She tries to win points off the most deadly serves. Margaret Court says that Evonne can be almost beaten, but she still tries to hit winners.

"She just won't play safe tennis," says Margaret. "Her shots are quite unpredictable. They're liable to come back in any direction. She never lets up trying to catch you on your wrong foot."

One reason tennis crowds adore Evonne is that she always smiles. She never gets upset or annoyed.

"I don't usually get angry at myself when I make a bad shot," she explains. "Tennis is fun for me. It should be fun for everyone who's watching, too. If I lose a match, it's not the end of the world."

Evonne is a relaxed, natural young woman. She plays golf for recreation. She likes clothes, parties, and nightclubs. And she also loves music. At night she listens to rock music on her transistor radio until she falls asleep. If she were not a tennis player, she'd like to be a musician. "My brother plays the guitar," she says. "I'd like to do that."

In June, 1975, Evonne married Roger Cawley, a twenty-five-year-old British businessman.

Several times a year Evonne returns to Barellan to visit her family, but she never stays more than a few days.

"It's nice country, but it's too slow for me now," she says. "Tennis is my whole life. I could not imagine any other."

FIVE
Mighty Mouse: Margaret Court

"Hey, this is private property!" the man shouted. "Go along and don't let me catch you again!"

Wally Rutter, owner of the Albury Tennis Club, looked angry. A hundred times he had chased those youngsters away. A hundred times they'd come back. He knew they crept under the back fence. He was always yelling at the gang of boys and one spindly girl, who looked about ten.

Actually the spindly girl was eight, but Margaret Smith was tall for her age.

Margaret was born in the small town of Albury in Australia. Her father worked in a butter and cheese factory. As a child she never liked the games girls played. Instead she preferred to tag along with her three older brothers. She was happiest playing football and cricket.

Nobody in her family played tennis, but some of the boys in her neighborhood did. They thought it was fun to sneak into the Albury Tennis Club. There was one court in the corner almost surrounded by hedges. As long as the ball didn't bounce off the court, nobody could see them.

It was Margaret's job to stand at the net and hit back every ball. If she missed, the ball would roll away and they were sure to be caught.

Margaret learned to hit fairly well, but many times they were caught anyway. After a while, Wally Rutter tired of chasing them away. He also began to notice something. Margaret was good at the game. In fact, she was very good. When she was ten, he began giving her lessons on Saturday mornings.

As a teenager, Margaret enjoyed dancing and reading detective stories, watching television and going to the movies, but tennis began taking up more and more of her free time.

Wally could see that she was awkward and painfully shy, but he thought she had talent. He mentioned her to several tennis coaches. "She could be a champion someday," he said, "but first she needs a lot of training."

One of Wally's coach friends had been a Wimbledon champion. Frank Sedgman owned a gymnasium in Melbourne, one of Australia's biggest cities. He invited Margaret to spend a few months there. She could work as a receptionist at his gym, and he would teach her all he knew about tennis.

First, however, he wanted to make her stronger. He worried that she was too frail for tennis. "You have to get some muscle on those bones," he was always telling her.

Margaret's training schedule was tough. She exercised on the bars and trampolines. She jumped rope endlessly. She lifted weights. Soon she could lift 150 pounds.

She also ran for miles. The first time she ran the 220-yard dash, she covered the distance in 26 seconds. Her speed equaled the world's record at that time. Frank was

impressed. He realized that she could be a fine athlete in any sport.

"Maybe you should try out for the Olympic team," he suggested.

Margaret thought for a while. Being an Olympic runner sounded nice, but she liked tennis better.

"I just want to be the best tennis player I can," she told him.

Meanwhile Margaret had begun entering tournaments for junior players. She beat everybody she played, and collected more than fifty trophies.

When she was seventeen, she entered the Australian singles championship, the most important tournament in her country. She reached the final where she defeated Jan Le Hane, 7-5, 6-2. Overnight she became a celebrity in Australia. She was not prepared for fame, however.

Margaret had always been terribly shy. Now she began to suffer from nervousness. Playing before a crowd scared her. When she walked out on the court, she became filled with dread.

"I didn't learn to relax and really enjoy tennis until much later," she recalls. Even much later, however, she still was troubled by nerves.

After winning the Australian title, she wanted to go to Europe for other big competitions. Frank Sedgman said no, she wasn't ready yet. He wanted her to conquer her anxiety.

The following year she traveled to Italy, France, and England. In every tournament, Margaret reached the quarterfinals or semifinals. Encouraged, she began spending much of her time abroad.

In 1962 she won the United States title at Forest Hills. In

1963 she played at Wimbledon and won. She defeated Billie Jean Moffit, 6-3, 6-4. She also won the Australian title for the third year in a row.

By this time, she was learning to control her fears. "When you are at the top," she said then, "all the pressures on you can make you nervous and that definitely affects my concentration."

She forced herself to watch the ball, to think about her next move. She began wearing less glamorous tennis dresses. Simple, tailored clothes made her feel more comfortable.

Margaret worked hard and continued to win. In 1965 she captured both the American and Wimbledon titles. That year she began to think about her life. She had won nearly everything, but she wasn't happy.

Eight months of the year she was away from home. She got tired of traveling, of packing and unpacking suitcases. She was even a little bored with chasing tennis balls. So at twenty-four she decided to give up tennis.

Margaret and a friend opened a dress shop in Perth. They sold sportswear and teenage dresses. Perth is a lovely city on the west coast of Australia. Life there was relaxing. During her teens, Margaret had missed the usual parties and friendships. Now she tried to make up for her loss.

After a few months in Perth, she met Barry Court, a yachtsman and wool broker. They were soon married.

Margaret had no plans to return to tennis, but Barry thought they could have fun traveling around the world together. "Marg, I want you to quit whenever you want," Barry said, "but not for my sake. Only when you're satisfied you've gotten everything from tennis."

There was something she wanted from tennis—a Grand Slam. That means winning the four big championships all in one year—Australia, France, England (Wimbledon), and the United States. Very few players had done it and only one woman, Maureen Connolly.

When Margaret returned to tennis in 1968, she had not played for nearly two years. It took her almost an entire season to regain her skill, but eventually she was playing better than before.

She also enjoyed touring more. Having Barry with her made a big difference. "It was so nice to have somebody there with me when I stopped playing for the day," she says, "someone to share it with."

By 1970 she was in brilliant form. That year, she vowed to try for a Grand Slam. First she took the Australian championship. Then there was the French Open, which she won easily.

Next came Wimbledon. Early in the tournament she slipped and tore an ankle ligament. By the time she met Billie Jean King in the final, her ankle was badly swollen. She played fiercely just the same. The match lasted two hours and twenty-seven minutes. Finally she managed to overcome Billie Jean.

Now all that stood between Margaret and the Grand Slam was the American title. At Forest Hills she sailed through the quarterfinals and semifinals. In the final she would be facing Rosemary Casals.

On the morning of September 13, 1970, she rose early and ate a quick breakfast. Then she went to church. She and Barry took a subway from their hotel in New York City to the stadium at Forest Hills.

During the first set Margaret played badly. She made several errors and quite a few bad shots. Still, she squeaked through to win, 6-2. Rosie took the second set, 2-6. It began to look as if Margaret had lost her Grand Slam.

There was a ten-minute break. When Margaret returned to the court, she wore a determined look. She began to attack Rosie with strong forehand shots.

"Margaret's arms seemed to be all over the court," Rosie said later.

In the third set Margaret overwhelmed Rosie, 6-1. The match was over and the Grand Slam belonged to her!

In 1971 she left tennis to have a child. No woman player had ever come back after a baby, but the next year Margaret returned with a racket in one hand and a baby bottle in the other. From then on, her family accompanied her wherever she went. While she played, Barry baby-sat with little Danny.

Soon after her second comeback, Margaret suffered an embarrassing defeat. Bobby Riggs had challenged several women to an exhibition match. All of them refused. Margaret accepted. The match was set for Mother's Day in Ramona, California.

Riggs was familiar with Margaret's career. Before the match, he outlined his strategy. "The only reason she lost a major match in the last ten years was that she would get uptight," he said. "So this will be a war of nerves."

A reporter asked Margaret if she had a strategy. Margaret shrugged. "Not particularly," she replied. "He doesn't hit the ball that hard anymore."

If there was one thing she could do, it was hit the ball hard. Margaret is a big woman, 5'9" and 157 pounds. She is also very strong. Once scientists tested her and found that she is stronger than most men.

With her mighty serves and volleys, she is said to play like a man. Other women players call her 'Mighty Mouse.'

Mother's Day did not begin well for Margaret. First her baby son threw her favorite pair of sneakers into the toilet. Then Riggs presented her with a bouquet of red roses accompanied by a note that said: "Women are not only the weaker sex but, as athletes, the dumber one."

Margaret never recovered. Only fifty-seven minutes later, Riggs won, 6-2, 6-1. Afterward he called the match 'The Mother's Day Massacre.' Margaret refused to talk about it.

The Riggs match was a disaster, but the rest of the year was one of her best. She won the championships in Australia, France, and the United States—three of the Big Four. She also collected over $200,000 in prize money.

The next year she retired again. She had another child, a daughter, but when the 1975 season opened, Margaret was back.

At the age of thirty-two, Margaret had achieved an extraordinary record. She had won more major tournaments than any other player—man or woman—in the history of tennis. She also managed to combine her career with marriage and motherhood.

"I respect what Women's Lib is doing in some things," she says, "but I'm not Women's Lib. I'm just a wife and mother who plays tennis. For me, my family comes first."

ABOUT THE AUTHOR

Marion Meade is a well-known feminist who has written both adult and juvenile books on the subject of women. Her articles have appeared in a wide range of newspapers and magazines including *The New York Times*, the *Village Voice*, *McCalls*, *Cosmopolitan*, and others. She received a B.S. from Northwestern University and an M.S. from Columbia Graduate School of Journalism. Ms. Meade lives in New York City with her eight-year-old daughter and twelve-year-old Scottie. She is an avid tennis fan.